Mammals in the Wild

Tigers

by Kathryn Clay

PEBBLE
a capstone imprint

Pebble Books are published by Pebble
1710 Roe Crest Drive, North Mankato,
Minnesota 56003
www.mycapstone.com

Library of Congress Cataloging-in-Publication Data
Names: Clay, Kathryn, author.
Title: Tigers : a 4D book / by Kathryn Clay.
Description: North Mankato, Minnesota : an imprint of
    Pebble, [2019] | Series: Little Pebble. Mammals in the
    wild | Audience: Age 4-7.
Identifiers: LCCN 2018004133 (print) | LCCN 2018009138
    (ebook) | ISBN 9781977100887 (eBook PDF) | ISBN
    9781977100764 (hardcover) | ISBN 9781977100825
    (paperback)
Subjects: LCSH: Tiger—Juvenile literature.
Classification: LCC QL737.C23 (ebook) | LCC QL737.C23
    C536 2019 (print) | DDC 599.756—dc23
LC record available at https://lccn.loc.gov/2018004133

Editorial Credits
Karen Aleo, editor; Juliette Peters, designer;
Tracy Cummins and Heather Mauldin, media researchers;
Laura Manthe, production specialist

Photo Credits
Getty Images: Picture by Tambako the Jaguar, 11;
Newscom: Theo Allofs/Minden Pictures, 17; Shutterstock:
Dzmitry Kim, Design Element, George Lamson, 21,
Nachiketa Bajaj, Cover, Natasha Zalevskaya Design
Element, neelsky, 13, niall dunne, 19, Pablo77, 15, Richard
Constantinoff, 7, Sarah Cheriton-Jones, 5, Tiago Jorge da
Silva Estima, 1, Yvdalmia, 9

Table of Contents

At Home

A big cat lies in the grass.

It's a tiger!

Tigers are mammals.

Mammals have hair or fur.

They have warm blood.

Tigers can be found in forests.
Others live in tall grass.

Big Cats

Tigers have big paws.

Their claws are sharp.

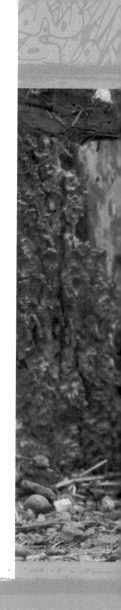

Tigers have orange fur.

They also have dark stripes.

Each stripe is different.

Tigers wait.

They hide behind bushes.

Tigers hunt.

Roar!

A tiger leaps.

It chases the prey.

Baby Tigers

Look!

Here are two cubs.

They start out small.

Cubs drink milk.

They grow up fast.

Glossary

claw—a hard curved nail on the foot of an animal

cub—a young tiger

forest—land filled with trees that grow
close together

hunt—to find and catch animals for food

leap—to jump a long way

mammal—a warm-blooded animal that breathes air;
mammals have hair or fur; female mammals feed
milk to their young

paws—the feet of animals with four feet and claws

prey—an animal hunted by another animal
for food

Read More

Archer, Claire. *Tigers. Big Cats.* Minneapolis: Abdo Kids, 2014.

Hall, Margaret. *Tigers and Their Cubs: A 4D Book.* Animal Offspring. North Mankato, Minn.: Capstone Press, 2018.

Statts, Leo. *Tigers.* Savanna Animals. Minneapolis: Abdo Zoom, 2017.

Internet Sites

Use FactHound to find Internet sites related to this book.

Visit www.facthound.com

Just type in 9781977100764 and go.

Check out projects, games and lots more at
www.capstonekids.com

Critical Thinking Questions

1. Adult tigers catch prey. What does prey mean?
2. Where do tigers live?
3. What do cubs drink?

Index